# Gratitude

Publications International, Ltd.

**Contributing writers:** Janice Deal, Marie D. Jones

**Cover art:** Shutterstock.com

**Interior art:** Shutterstock.com except 11, 87, 90, 132, 139, 158, 186, 252 from Getty

Louis Weber, CEO
Publications International, Ltd.
7373 North Cicero Avenue
Lincolnwood, Illinois 60712

ISBN: 978-1-68022-320-0

Manufactured in China.

8 7 6 5 4 3 2 1

# To give thanks is good.

**—Algernon Charles Swinburne**

*So often we rush through our days, trying to mark off items on our to-do list. Then we look back and wonder how the day, the season, or the year went so quickly. When we make an effort as we move through the day to be mindful and aware of the present moment, we find ourselves slowing down and savoring the events of our lives.*

*The practice of mindfulness has many rewards—it can deepen our relationships and bolster our mental, physical, and emotional health. It can also lead us to realize how much we have for which to be grateful. And cultivating the habit of feeling and expressing gratitude can renew our appreciation for our family members, our friends, the beauty of nature, and so much more.*

*This book reflects on a few of the many things for which you might be grateful. The old saying goes, "Stop and smell the roses." But even when you don't see roses around, take some time to stop and look around you. You may be surprised by how much beauty you find!*

Gratitude lifts the spirit and warms the heart.

Gratitude opens doors to new perspectives.

Gratitude reminds us we are never alone.

Gratitude connects us to everything and
everyone around us.

Gratitude removes blocks to happiness by
keeping our focus in the here and now.

*I never realized the power of making a gratitude list when nothing was going right. With financial stresses and my son suffering from health issues, it seemed there was little I could put on that list. But every night before I went to sleep, I forced myself to write down five good things that had happened that day. Sometimes they were small things, and inconsequential to anyone but me. But soon my lists were well over five. My lists today often surpass 20 things to be grateful for.*

*G*ratitude is an attitude of loving what you have, and this undoubtedly leads to having even more. When you open your eyes to the bountiful blessings already in your life, you realize just how abundant the world really is. Suddenly, you feel more giving, more loving, and more open to even greater blessings. Gratitude is a key that unlocks the door to treasures you already have, and it yields greater treasures yet to be discovered.

6

*The secret of happiness is not found in seeking more, but in developing the capacity to enjoy less.*

—Socrates

*Have nothing in your house that you do not know to be useful, or believe to be beautiful.*

—William Morris

$\mathcal{T}$ime spent with an old friend who's come into town for a visit is a gift. With old friends, even if we don't talk regularly, we can pick up where we left off in sharing news, unburdening ourselves, and reminiscing about the past. Old friendships develop a kind of shorthand over the years, where a few words can invoke a rich piece of shared history. Our oldest friends have a deep knowledge of us and how we have changed and grown over the years. How beautiful it is to be truly known and loved, flaws and all, over the course of years.

*Keep your friendship in repair.*

—Ralph Waldo Emerson

*Friendship is a sheltering tree.*

—Samuel Taylor Coleridge

*The best mirror is an old friend.*

—George Herbert

Want to be happier and less stressed out? Scientists at the University of Berkeley's Greater Good Science Center have found that making a daily list of three things you are grateful for works wonders. There is no need to go on a long silent retreat, when doing something as simple as focusing on a handful of things to be grateful for is enough to lower stress and make you smile more.

*Rainy days bring such delights to the senses.*

*The soothing sound of rain on the ground.*

*The rich smell of freshly nourished earth.*

*The dark skies hiding the return of the sun.*

*The laughter of children jumping in puddles.*

*The world around us cleansed and refreshed.*

*The clouds morphing into shapes.*

*I am grateful for rainy days.*

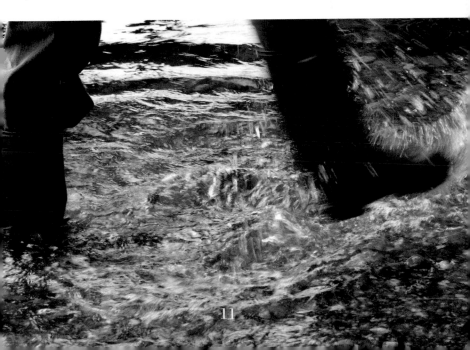

*P*lans energize us and fill us with hope. Whether we decide to have friends over for soup and homemade bread, or paint the baseboard a cheerful yellow, our plans demand creativity, our energy, and our joy. By giving us a goal, or something to look forward to, plans uplift us. Let us celebrate them!

Family is our foundation, our roots,

and our source of identity.

Family loves us through the best

times and the worst times.

Family gets us—our quirks, our

jokes, our wit and wisdom.

Family always tells it to us straight.

Family means we are never alone

in the world.

Family is where the heart is,

and where we call home.

$\mathcal{I}$ hadn't ridden a bicycle in years, but when my daughter received a bike for her birthday, I had my old 10-speed tuned up and we began to ride together. I had forgotten how one notices things that can be overlooked by car. A house with blue shutters. The cat lounging on a stone step. Today I celebrate bicycles, and the mindfulness they encourage!

*I* wandered lonely as a cloud
That floats on high o'er vales and hills,
When all at once I saw a crowd,
A host, of golden daffodils.

—William Wordsworth

*Summer afternoon—summer afternoon; to me those words have always been the two most beautiful words in the English language.*

—Henry James

*Blessings are always found in lessons.*

*Be grateful for challenges in life that*

*stretch us beyond our comfort zone.*

*Give thanks for difficult times that make*

*us appreciate the good times more.*

*Have gratitude towards difficult people*

*who teach us about ourselves.*

*Be thankful for pain and suffering that*

*is followed by hope, healing, and joy.*

*Live with thanks for every*

*experience life gives us.*

Gratitude may make you more moral. That's what a 1988 study in the *British Journal of Social Psychology* showed. People who experienced gratitude were more likely to behave in moral ways, and to be more likely to help their fellow humans as well. Being grateful also led to more desire to volunteer and help people (including strangers) because of a greater concern for others.

What work has gone into bridges over the years! Some of the ancient Roman bridges are still in use today, centuries later. These feats of engineering are often taken for granted, until we think of the thought and care that went into their design and building. They remind us of what humans can achieve through work, imagination, and cooperation.

*Do what you can, with what you have,
where you are.*

—Theodore Roosevelt

*Happiness lies not in the mere possession
of money; it lies in the joy of achievement,
in the thrill of creative effort.*

—Franklin D. Roosevelt

German philosopher and poet Johann Wolfgang von Goethe was interested in science and the study of forms; in particular, he celebrated the classification of clouds as dictated by young meteorologist Luke Howard. Cumulus. Stratus. Cirrus. Nimbus. The names alone excite the spirit! Goethe was so inspired by clouds, he wrote a series of poems about their energy and diversity, and I appreciate his fascination. Today I commemorate clouds in all their transitory beauty!

Four ducks on a pond,

A grass-bank beyond,

A blue sky of spring,

White clouds on the wing:

What a little thing

To remember for years—

To remember with tears!

—William Allingham

$\mathcal{T}$here is no reason such delight can bring,

As summer, autumn, winter, and the spring.

—William Browne

$\mathcal{D}$affodils,

That come before the swallow dares, and take

The winds of March with beauty.

—William Shakespeare

$\mathcal{G}$ive thanks for the colorful blooms of spring, for the migration of birds and the appearance of butterflies. Enjoy how the scenery seems to change every day as leaves bud and trees become green once more. On stormy days, stop and appreciate the clouds scudding across the sky, the smell of rain, and the sudden crack of lightning.

oday I pledge to walk mindfully. May I appreciate the mystery of my body, the way I can move. May I take in the weather around me and really focus on the touch of the wind, the brightness of the sky. May I feel the earth beneath my feet. May I feel gratitude for the simple act of walking.

A University of North Carolina study tells us to think positive! The study looked at positive thoughts and attitudes as more than just being upbeat. It showed that being of a positive mindset actually adds value to life and helps you build skills like finding more options for a challenge, and seeing more possibilities to lead to a happier outcome.

Inebriate of Air—am I—

And Debauchee of Dew—

Reeling —through endless summer days—

From inns of Molten Blue—

—Emily Dickinson

Give thanks for summer, for the sunny skies and the long evenings, for corn on the cob and peaches, for lazy days on the beach. When the weather is sweltering, be grateful for all the things that keep you cool, iced tea, fresh fruit, and air conditioning. Give thanks for the activities of summer, festivals and fairs and summer camps where kids can learn crafts and go on nature hikes and build robots.

*O* suns and skies and clouds of June,

And flowers of June together,

Ye cannot rival for one hour

October's bright blue weather

—Helen Hunt Jackson

The joys of autumn are many. For some, autumn is all about hikes through a local forest preserve to see the leaves change brilliant colors. For others, it's about the return of foods and drinks flavored with pumpkin spice! For parents and kids, autumn brings a flurry of back-to-school activities and fresh possibilities—new school supplies and teachers and things to learn. What have your autumns brought you?

_O_ world, I cannot hold thee close enough!

Thy winds, thy wide grey skies!

Thy mists that roll and rise!

Thy woods, this autumn day, that ache and sag

And all but cry with colour! That gaunt crag

To crush! To lift the lean of that black bluff!

World, World, I cannot get thee close enough!

—Edna St. Vincent Millay

Whatever form Thanksgiving takes, whether it's a big celebration with family or an informal potluck with friends, whether you're eating turkey or chicken curry, take a few moments to be thankful for your hosts or your guests, the food you're eating and the people who prepared it.

Give me the end of the year an' its fun

When most of the plannin' an' toilin' is done;

Bring all the wanderers home to the nest,

Let me sit down with the ones I love best,

Hear the old voices still ringin' with song,

See the old faces unblemished by wrong,

See the old table with all of its chairs

An' I'll put soul in my Thanksgivin' prayers.

—Edgar Albert Guest

Give thanks for warmth on cold days, for an hour spent in front of the fireplace with a good book, homemade quilts and afghans, and the taste of hot chocolate after a round of snow shoveling. Relish hand-knit sweaters, colorful mittens, a hearty stew cooking in the slow cooker. Delight in a furnace that works, puffy coats, and comfy slippers.

It is the time of year when the sun shines warm during the day, but temperatures drop at night. Yesterday was a long day, and when I returned home I was cold and tired. I pulled out a favorite sweater, remembering the day I bought it with my beloved late mom. The sweater warmed me, both physically and emotionally. I am grateful for clothing and the comfort it brings!

*A single kind word can warm three winter months.*

—Anonymous

*No one can look at a pine tree in winter without knowing that spring will come again in due time.*

—Frank Bolles

Give thanks for the beauty found on the coldest days of winter in frost patterns and pristine snow banks, for the joy found in hurtling downhill on sleds or skis, for the happiness found in watching children making snowmen and snow angels. And don't forget to give thanks for those who shovel snow and plow streets and parking lots!

$\mathcal{E}$ven that old horse

is something to see

this snow-covered morning.

—Matsuo Basho

$\mathcal{T}$hus having prepared their buds

against a sure winter

the wise trees

stand sleeping in the cold.

—William Carlos Williams

Want more joy and contentment out of life? Think about the good stuff. Positive thoughts, including gratitude, improve our chances of seeing the good in any situation and help us navigate life much more skillfully. That's what research by positive psychology researcher Barbara Frederickson has suggested. The attitude of gratitude is a ticket to a happier life.

There is always something to be grateful for.

The taste of coffee first thing in the morning.

An email from a long lost friend.

A check in the mail for a job well done.

The sound of birds outside your window as you work.

Bacon sizzling on the stove.

A favorite shirt you can't live without.

Your loved ones sitting around the dinner table.

Being alive.

Cooking is a form of creativity. It is a way of showing love. When our friends come over and we prepare a meal, there is communion and industry. Over the table, we share stories and news. The good food nourishes us and motivates us to gather. I am grateful for cooking!

Showing gratitude on a regular basis, such as weekly or daily, can have positive benefits on everything from achieving more goals, exercising more, and being more aware and alert, according to a series of studies done in 2003. Being grateful is something we can do at any time, but making it a regular practice is good for the body, mind, and spirit.

Listening is a powerful tool. In our fast-paced society, we don't always slow down enough to understand what another is saying; so many times we are already thinking ahead to what we want to say next. And yet when I take the time to listen, I connect more deeply with my loved ones. Sometimes I learn something new. I am grateful for listening, and the gifts it can bestow.

The quality of a friendship can be measured by the amount of silence the two of you are comfortable letting pass between you when you are together.

*It is a great thing to know the season for speech and the season for silence.*

—Seneca

Material objects are wonderful, but often we get too attached to them and become jealous of those who have more. Interestingly, a 2001 study showed that people who described themselves as more grateful experienced less materialistic feelings of jealousy and envy. They also understood that material success and objects were not an important source of happiness.

Our connections to others enrich us. We can be alone in a room, and yet, because of the myriad relationships in our lives, feel safe and sustained. We know there is a loved one, a dear friend, to whom we might reach out. There is comfort in connection.

It can be hard to think about relationships and friendships that have ended, through conflict or because of a slow drifting apart as interests and lives diverged. We remember the endings with sadness or disappointment.

But we can look, too, at the friendship as a whole, and be grateful—for the good times shared, hobbies learned or books and music that were introduced, for the ways we grew or were changed for the better.

Flowers are lovely; love is flower-like;

Friendship is a sheltering tree.

—Samuel Taylor Coleridge

$\mathcal{I}$ am grateful for the evenings when we've gathered with friends after dinner to play a board game. Conversation flows in a way it doesn't if we've stationed ourselves in front of the television. There is a give-and-take, and there is laughter. I appreciate how games draw people together, and how they can challenge us: sometimes games even help us to develop new skills!

*Without friends
no one would
choose to live,
though he had
all other goods.*

—Aristotle

We don't like to appear foolish, to make mistakes in front of others. We like to have our act together—or at least to give the appearance that we do.

But sometimes when we make mistakes in front of others, we experience the gift of kindness in return. The stranger who helps pick up a dropped stack of paper, the colleague who gently corrects an error during your first months at work, the friend who forgives a slip of the tongue—because of their generosity of spirit, we can even be grateful for our own vulnerability.

*All experience is an arch*
*to build upon.*

—Henry Brooks Adams

*H*ave you had a kindness shown?

Pass it on.

—Henry Burton

*H*ow wonderful it is to live in an era where we can access so many kinds of music so easily! Today's technology makes it simple to explore different genres, to find new artists, and to point our friends to a song we love.

What songs are you glad to have heard? What moments that involve music are you glad to remember? What songs make you want to sing along?

$\mathcal{M}$usic can:

Lift our hearts

Provide catharsis

Bind us together

Voice our unspoken thoughts

Move us to dance

*Musick is the thing of the world that I love most.*

—Samuel Pepys

When I wake in the morning, I have a reason for being: my children, fulfilling work, friends and family, and the clay mugs I make on a wheel. I tend my garden. I prepare meals with care. I am grateful for purpose, which grants my life meaning. I am lucky.

*Then do not grasp at the stars, but do life's plain, common work as it comes, certain that daily duties and daily bread are the sweetest things in life.*

—Robert Louis Stevenson

*It is the sweet, simple things of life which are the real ones after all.*

—Laura Ingalls Wilder

$\mathcal{A}$ pastime that involves silence and little action can be a balm to the soul. Along with competitive sports, self-improvement, and workout routines, let's not forget gardening, fishing, sunbathing, and stargazing. Doing nothing but appreciating what's around us—is any hobby easier or more rewarding?

*I love fishing. I can think of no greater pleasure than to sit alone toward evening by the water and watch a float.*

—Anton Chekov

*Dwell on the beauty of life. Watch the stars and see yourself running with them.*

—Marcus Aurelius

*I cannot endure to waste anything so precious as autumnal sunshine by staying in the house.*

—Nathaniel Hawthorne

Mountains figure in literature, movies, and song; they call to us with their fresh air and pine smells. They offer such beauty, from the blue fog lingering over the Great Smoky Mountains to the sharply delineated peaks of the Sawtooth range. We can hike or ski, and the exercise uplifts us. Spend a day in the mountains and sleep comes easy.

$\mathcal{I}$ try to eat healthfully, and like the way I feel when I do. And yet, variety uplifts us: there is nothing like dessert to complement a meal every now and again. Sweet things can be fun, and they give me a lift. Butter cake crusted with sugar, colorful iced pastries bursting with cream: I love and celebrate them all today!

The sweetness of ice cream threaded with chocolate. The dark, nutty flavor of coffee, or a salad that tastes like spring. Our taste buds bring every meal, every snack, to life. Bitter, sweet, sour, salt, and umami, a Japanese word that describes savory: the five tastes evoke worlds.

Today I celebrate habits, both good and bad. Good habits keep me on a healthy track, of course: when I eat right or exercise regularly, my life is improved. But even bad habits have their place, because they pose a challenge to overcome, a way for me to grow as a person. I am glad for habits, which shape and help me become my best self.

*W*hen we go to an art museum, we learn about history (think Picasso's *Guernica*). We are reminded of the beauty of nature (Henri Rousseau's jungle paintings are a marvel). Art, whether painting or sculpture or installation piece, challenges us to contemplate the human condition, and invites us to open our minds and hearts.

Recent scientific studies show that
being more grateful not only makes
us happier, less isolated, and more
compassionate, but it also lowers
blood pressure and strengthens the
immune system. Consistent gratitude
practice of some kind improves levels
of optimism, which leads to more joy.
Gratitude is medicine for the soul.

My brain controls my body temperature—it allows me to move, learn, and love. It's also key to my consciousness—who I am as a person. I am a bit awed by the human brain, which is so complex and powerful that scientists are still working to understand it.

The famous Mayo Clinic has looked into positive mindsets and thinking, and the results are stunning. Positive thinking has many health benefits, including a longer life span, lower rates of stress and depression, a stronger immune system, better coping skills, increased psychological well-being, and even a lower rate of heart disease. Be positive, be grateful, be well!

$\mathcal{T}$oday I celebrate color: the rich tones of the brown leather couch where I write and read; the sunset hue of peaches in a wooden bowl; the cheerful lime green of the plastic wristwatch I bought on a whim. Color informs our days, and can uplift us. Our world is bright!

*A beautiful view. A mouthwatering meal. A movie that inspires, or a project successfully completed. When we share pleasures or projects, we bond with others and create meaningful interactions. We enjoy the satisfaction of working toward a common goal. Shared pleasures enhance life.*

Today I give grudging thanks for the challenges in my life. The difficult cousin with whom I must learn to get along; the work project outside my wheelhouse; the stubborn tub drain that refuses to unclog. Life's trials teach me patience and they help me grow. I do not always like challenge, but I am a better person for it!

Being more optimistic can make you a better problem solver, according to a study published in the journal *Health Psychology*. The power of positive thinking enables you to not only accept reality sooner, but to also get to work on finding ways to solve a problem or deal with a negative situation. Being more optimistic than pessimistic makes it easier to cope with the curveballs in the game of life.

Alone is not the same as lonely. Spending time alone can be an enjoyable experience; it can also be good for you. Making time for reflective thought boosts creativity and focus. Solitude also affords us the opportunity to recharge—to Just Be—in a fast-paced world.

$Q$uiet, steady adherence to goals leads to accomplishment. When we identify goals, when we work towards them with seriousness and determination, we are rewarded: with a job well done, a healthy child, a welcoming home. Let us honor what accomplishment represents, and its contribution to a life well lived.

Language is mystery! The symbols and sounds that help us communicate, also link us together and help us define the human experience. With language, we make sense of our experiences. We let others know how we feel and in turn learn about their worldviews, their way in the world. Language has power.

Words have power. If we are having a bad day—our coffeemaker broke, traffic was bad, our best friend had to cancel lunch—but someone reaches out to encourage us, the small annoyances can disappear; our perspective changes. Whether we receive it or reach out to build up someone else, encouragement has the power to turn a day around.

It's not always good, but news keeps us connected to others. When we understand what is going on in our communities, our country, our world, when we ponder the conflicts and triumphs affecting mankind, we are invited to form an opinion. Sometimes we are invited to act. By keeping us engaged, news demands that we consider who we are and our role in the world —and that's good.

When we are free—to share ideas, to shape our own destinies—we are lucky. When we are blessed with the freedom health allows, we can do what we want when we want. Freedom allows us to express our best selves, to carve a path that works for us; freedom grants autonomy.

Emotional well-being may be as close as being grateful for something. UC Davis professor Robert Emmons has spent the last eight years studying the positive effects of feelings of gratitude, which is an attitude we can choose to engage in at any time. Once we give up being a victim, we start to feel more open and energized, and even improve our emotional and physical health in the process. We can go from feeling lonely and depressed to connected and inspired.

It's a gray day and the couch seems to be calling to us. We're tired. But while it may seem counterintuitive, when we exercise, our energy levels go up. Exercise produces endorphins, which make us feel happy. And that bike ride or jog around the block gets us outside in the fresh air. If we can make the effort and honor exercise, it can make us a little bit better at life!

$S$ome friends are excellent confidantes. They listen carefully and offer comfort when we're dealing with a problem. Some friends offer practical advice or concrete help—a ride to work when the car breaks down, a casserole during a time of illness, or gas money during financially hard times. Some friends offer distraction, taking us out to a movie or telling stories to make us laugh during a health scare.

Sometimes we expect our friendships to be "one size fits all," thinking that a true friend would provide whatever we needed in times of crisis. But if we look at what our friends can and do offer, instead of getting disappointed when they don't meet some unspoken expectation, we can truly appreciate their strengths and their generosity.

*A faithful friend is a strong defense: and he that hath found such an one hath found a treasure.*

—Ecclesiasticus 6:14

*What is a friend? A single soul dwelling in two bodies.*

—Aristotle

*I am grateful for someone who understands when the whole world doesn't.*

—Judy Lane

I started keeping a gratitude journal when my father died. Before then, I wasn't good about writing things down. But his death made me take pause. In the sadness and grief, I was just listing things I loved about my dad and our life together. But soon the list had changed into general reasons for being grateful.

I noticed writing things on my list made memories sharper and I was able to recall so many good moments. I was also grateful for the not so good ones, because of what they taught me. Just thinking about it wasn't enough. Writing it down helped enrich not just my memories of my past, but my hopes for the future.

The human body can't produce salt. Without it, our bodies become chemically unbalanced. We rely on salt to keep our muscles and nervous system functioning, and so it needs to be continually replenished. Good thing salt enhances the flavor of food! It is essential to life.

$\mathcal{E}$ven your daily commute can be an environmen

for gratitude! Don't dwell on the things that went

wrong or irritated you. Instead, look for the things

that went right: the parking space that opened up as

you arrived, the person who let you merge in traffic,

the bus that was on time.

Say thank you to someone today. Smile as you say it to a cashier or barista. Send a text to a friend thanking them for something they did for you. Tell a colleague you appreciated their work.

$\mathcal{I}$n the desert, animals and plants have evolved to survive in an environment of extremes. The roots of the velvet mesquite, a common shrub in the Sonoran Desert, can plunge more than 50 meters to access water sources. That's taller than an 11-story building! The nocturnal fennec fox, found in the Sahara of North Africa, sports large ears that help dissipate body heat. Today I honor the desert and the adaptability of its inhabitants.

We are all connected. And institutions devoted to taking care and helping our fellows— that remind us of our connectedness—are to be celebrated. Charities ennoble and uplift us all by promoting giving, cooperation, and social bonds. Let us celebrate charities: the kindness they encourage, and the interdependence they foster.

Change can be stressful, studies show. But because it's also a constant, we can learn to celebrate it. Change cultivates flexibility and open-mindedness. It is the catalyst for new experiences that help us flourish. And managing change instills self-confidence; we learn we may not be able to control external events, but that we can adapt to them, even grow stronger. Change can be good!

$\mathcal{L}$et us celebrate libraries! By providing access to information, libraries inform individuals. Through literacy or enrichment programs, they reach out to marginalized or disadvantaged citizens. Without judgment, libraries include in their collections the work of artists outside the mainstream; by their very nature, they encourage creativity and independent thinking. Libraries are a place of sanctuary.

$\mathcal{W}$e live in a culture of choice. With access to education, we can choose our livelihood. We choose how we dress and the look or attitude we want to convey. We choose our life partners, and in turn are chosen. We honor the freedom and responsibility that comes with choice.

When snow falls, soft as featherdown, the world is hushed. Cars make a shushing sound; our footsteps crunch. Perhaps we make a snowman, or a fort. Snowballs lace through the air! If we have milk, sugar, vanilla, and salt, we add clean snow to make ice cream. Snow is wonderment.

$\mathcal{W}$henever I use the delicate china teacups patterned with willow, I think of my maternal grandmother. She grew up with very little, but she knew how to celebrate the tradition of tea shared with loved ones. The cups were hers, and I celebrate their beauty and meaning. Antiques carry their own stories of the past even as they inform our present.

*Tea beckons us to enjoy quality
time with friends and loved ones,
and especially to rediscover the
art of relaxed conversation.*

—Dorothea Johnson

*There are few hours in life
more agreeable than the hour
dedicated to the ceremony
known as afternoon tea.*

—Henry James

Recycling: it's good for the environment. It preserves landfill space, and creates jobs. It protects wildlife. There's much to appreciate about recycling. When we recycle, we respect our planet. We honor the living things with which we share this beautiful world.

*We need the tonic of wildness . . . We can never have enough of nature.*

—Henry David Thoreau

*The clearest way into the Universe is through a forest wilderness.*

—John Muir

*What is it about the power of touch? When I hug my daughter, when a friend hugs me, there is communion and comfort. Hugs connect us, they lower blood pressure, they send calming messages to the brain. And whether we hug a loved one, a favorite pet, or even our teddy bear, the benefits are the same. I am grateful for hugs!*

$\mathcal{T}$hank you for people who share their wisdom. Sometimes I may think I know everything, but it is good to realize that there are many people who are smarter than me. What a gift to receive their guidance in my life! Help me to have a listening ear and always be grateful for those who want to help me.

$\mathcal{M}$any traditions consider birds to be winged spirits representing freedom, transcendence, and divinity. As for me, they just make me happy. I have a birdfeeder in my backyard, and I love to sit by the window with a cup of coffee, taking in the small dramas that play out among the sparrows and finches, the cardinals and jays. I am grateful for the color and beauty of birds.

*The world acquired a new interest when birds appeared, for the presence of birds at any time is magical in effect. They are magicians that transform every scene; make of every desert a garden of delights.*

—Charles C. Abbott

*I hope you love birds, too. It is economical. It saves going to Heaven.*

—Emily Dickinson

Children possess a natural curiosity. To kids, the world is new; childhood and adolescence are defined by a sense of discovery. Being with my children reminds me of the importance of that spirit of inquiry, and when I am with them I feel my own senses awakened. I am grateful for curiosity, which keeps my brain elastic and my spirit young.

*Love children especially, for like the angels they too are sinless, and they live to soften and purify our hearts, and as it were, to guide us.*

—Feodor Dostoevsky

*Children are certainly too good to be true.*

—Robert Louis Stevenson

$\mathcal{F}$inding it difficult to remember gratitude? For a month, make it a project to write down five people or events that made you grateful that day. The first few days might be difficult, but then you'll find that as you go through the day, you are keeping your eyes open for things to add to that day's gratitude list. By the end of the month, you might find that you don't want to stop at five items a day!

How exciting it is to see and hear the busy hum of a city! I am thankful for all the people who live and work in cities. They have created places that thrum with life and energy. Great things can come from that energy, and I am grateful for the experiences cities provide to all of us.

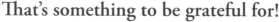

$\mathcal{H}$uman beings have apparently liked pillows for some time: in ancient China, pillows were functional but also beautiful, made of materials ranging from porcelain to wood. These days, we lay our heads on softer stuff, but the idea is the same: for many people, pillows provide support and comfort, and are part of a good night's sleep. That's something to be grateful for!

*Ever notice how the more grateful you are for the good things in your life, the more the floodgates tend to open, bringing even more good things? We lack for nothing when we are grateful for everything. That is when the blessings become a stream that never ceases to provide us with more to be grateful for*

In a world of change, routine can provide solace. Every morning I am the first to wake. I feed the cats, make the coffee, and then there is a quiet time when I enjoy my coffee from a pottery mug that feels smoothly weighted in my hand. I enjoy this tradition, and feel grateful for the peace it evokes.

*It is the appreciation of beauty and truth, the striving for knowledge, which makes life worth living.*

—Morris Raphael Cohen

*As we express our gratitude, we must never forget that the highest appreciation is not to utter words, but to live by them.*

—John F. Kennedy

*W*hat luck, to have someone come into our lives at just the right time to act as a mentor. Even as adults, we can learn so much from those who are older and wiser. Take some time to write a note of thanks to a person who has shared their wisdom and time with you.

*I can no other answer make,*
*but, thanks, and thanks.*

—William Shakespeare

*I would thank you from the*
*bottom of my heart, but for you*
*my heart has no bottom.*

—Unknown

Some days, we don't want to cook: we're tired, or short on time. Maybe we want to spend our time connecting with friends, rather than working in the kitchen. Restaurants allow us a respite from kitchen labors. When we eat out, we can relax, eat cuisines from around the world, and focus on conversation. Restaurants can be liberating!

*How* marvelous our bodies!
May we care for them today with all the
reverence and honor we might extend
toward any great gift that defies explanation.

*Our life is frittered away by detail . . . Simplify, simplify.*

—Henry David Thoreau

$\mathcal{M}$anifest plainness.

Embrace simplicity.

Reduce selfishness.

Have few desires.

—Lao-tzu

*Live simply, so others may simply live.*

—Mahatma Gandhi

In a busy life, I am grateful for those times when I can slow down. I turn off the radio and put my technology away. I sit quietly, with or without a book, and become engaged with my surroundings. The rumble of a truck passing by. The spring smell of grass. A lampshade's soft glow. I am quiet, and my heart is full.

Linda was furious about losing the promotion. She'd worked hard for it. She went home depressed and angry. A friend suggested looking for the "blessing in the lesson," but to Linda, there was none. But she thought about it and realized the promotion would have meant more hours and not much more pay.

The more Linda dwelled on the good things about losing the promotion, the more grateful she felt for her own job. On the following day she was thrilled to find her boss waiting, with news of a nice raise. Linda smiled, grateful for how it all worked out perfectly.

The moon controls the tides. She lights the night. She is our moon, waxing and waning in the night skies, and exciting our admiration and awe over the millennia. Let us celebrate the beauty and mystery of the moon's bright face!

$\mathcal{E}$ssential, seemingly invisible plumbing: we don't think of it until the pipes freeze, or the sink backs up. But every day I exalt in a hot shower; just one turn of a faucet, and I can effortlessly fill the kettle for tea. Today I celebrate the homely joys of plumbing.

To live in anger erodes the soul. I am grateful for forgiveness: when I can let go of my own outrage and forgive another, I am loosed from anger's prison. And I am humbled and grateful when my own mistakes are forgiven. Forgiveness frees us to connect, to try again, to be our best selves.

My ancestors came to America via Ellis Island during the 1920s. They came with nothing but the clothes on their backs and the dreams in their hearts. The stories I've heard of what they experienced make me proud and grateful.

Without their suffering, we might not be as blessed as we are today. I am filled with such gratitude for what my great-grandparents and grandparents endured so that my generation could have the lives we enjoy now. Our ancestors paved the way for us to have more access to our own American dreams. I am grateful for their sacrifices.

With a grateful heart, I appreciate what is.

Every challenge brings the gift of wisdom.

Every obstacle strengthens my resolve.

Every difficulty sweetens the good times.

Every blessing leads to deeper appreciation.

Every opportunity offers new possibilities.

Every abundance gives me more to share.

Every sorrow leads to joy tomorrow.

Every joyful moment reminds me how I am deeply loved.

$\mathcal{B}$alance: not always easy to achieve, and yet I am joyful when I manage it. Time with loved ones, time for meaningful work, time to be active, time to be quiet: I am grateful for the days when balance can be struck!

$\mathcal{T}$oday I will strive to celebrate little things: the particular way sun lights up a wood floor; the sharp sweetness of a lemon muffin; the feel of a cotton sweater against my neck. Big achievements or joys do not happen every day, but if I am mindful, each day affords its small pleasures; little things, so often overlooked, can contribute to deep satisfaction.

*Today, I am grateful for:*

*Another day to be alive and living my life.*

*Another opportunity to love those who are special to me.*

*Another chance to share my love with strangers I meet.*

*Another set of lessons to learn and wisdom to be gleaned.*

*Another blessing of clearing out the old and welcoming the new*

*Another experience of the awe and wonder of nature.*

On a Sunday afternoon, we recharge for the week ahead. Perhaps we read a book, or take a walk with a friend. We can look ahead to work or school, but not yet fully dive in. Sunday afternoons have their pleasures.

The plus side of being ill is realizing how good it feels to be well. I got one of the worst flu bugs last fall and was literally bedridden for a week with high fever, aches, and weakness. Worse still, my son got it, too. So not only was I sicker than I'd ever been, but I had to care for my child.

As bad as I felt, I was grateful for every moment I felt good enough to get up and walk around. I felt gratitude for having my son to care for and snuggle with. And when I started recuperating, I was overwhelmed with how good it felt. We only appreciate our health when it's taken away from us!

*I am grateful for the past and all it taught me.*

*I am blessed with memories of loved ones*

*come and gone.*

*I am devoted to carrying on my*

*family traditions.*

*I give thanks to those who worked hard to*

*make my life better.*

*I cherish the stories that make up who I am*

*and where I came from.*

*I am grateful for the wisdom and experience*

*I've gained.*

$\mathcal{H}$umans are drawn to waterfalls, their beauty and their power. Hearing the roar of a great cascade, seeing water tumble over rock, how can we be anything but amazed? What a joy to see that sight!

Great wide, beautiful, wonderful world,

With the wonderful waters round you curled,

And the wonderful grass upon your breast,

World, you are beautifully dressed.

—William Brighty Rands

If only the world

were always like this—

some fishermen

drawing a little boat

onto the river's bank.

—Minamoto no Sanetomo

As an artist, Gemma struggled to make ends meet. She entered her work in contests, gave pieces to local restaurants for free, and asked friends to spread the word. But when she decided to try crowdfunding as a last resort, she got a surprise lesson.

Gemma wanted to raise five thousand dollars to go to Italy to learn from a professional painter who was holding a seminar there. Instead, she ended up with donations totaling over ten thousand, most from total strangers. Gemma was grateful for the support, even if it came cloaked in mystery.

They're a "want," not a "need," but when we have a dishwasher, our lives are made exponentially easier. Those of us who like to cook also know how much mess can be generated in an inspired kitchen. Let us take a moment to celebrate the machine that washes our dishes so that we don't have to!

I was always in control of my life. But when events spiraled out of control, I didn't know how to cope. My health took a bad turn, my employer went bankrupt, and the love of my life cheated. I felt like life was over.

It took a good friend's perspective to help me realize even though things were falling apart, it was an opportunity for me create something new. And this time I wouldn't try to control it all. I was grateful to give up the need to micromanage my life and the lives of others. Suddenly, doors began to open and I felt hope again.

The day after a fresh haircut is an exhilarating one. I have short hair, and the clean lines of a new cut please me, as does the touch of air on my neck. I feel invigorated, spiffy, new. I feel so grateful for haircuts today!

Today there is rain. I celebrate the smell of it, and the way it nourishes my garden. I like the chalky blue-gray of the clouds. Today I am happy to stay inside, doing my work and reading a book. My cat is close by; the lamp shares its light in the rain-dim day. I am grateful.

$\mathcal{S}$omeday I hope to win a major award so I can thank you in front of a huge audience for all you've done. But for now these simple words of gratitude will have to do. Thank you, teacher, for believeing in me and never settling for less than my best.

Your attention made me feel important.

Your wisdom made me smarter.

Your support made me stronger.

Thank you, teacher, for caring enough to

see me succeed.

The range of human creativity is amazing: art, music, sculpture, flower arranging, quilting, architecture, jewelry, and so much more. People design and create so many beautiful things!

Look around at your own belongings. Be thankful for the ones that bring you joy and the work that went into them.

*Art washes away from the soul the dust of everyday life.*

—Pablo Picasso

*This world . . . is still a miracle; wonderful, inscrutable, magical, and more, to whosoever will think of it.*

—Thomas Carlyle

Poetry helps us see the world differently. It can be concise and yet pack a punch, getting to the heart of human experience with perception and grace. I like the way it expresses familiar sentiments in an unfamiliar way. Sometimes, it seems like singing. Today I celebrate poetry and the way it challenges and uplifts me.

*Arranging a bowl of flowers in the morning can give a sense of quiet in a crowded day—like writing a poem, or saying a prayer.*

—Anne Morrow Lindbergh

*Nothing is worth more than this day.*

—Johann Wolfgang von Goethe

Isn't it funny how Halloween candy can make us feel cheerful? Maybe it's the whimsy of bite-sized candy bars in their colorful foil wraps. Maybe it's the way candy corn looks, striping a pretty jar. Peanut butter cups are suddenly shaped like pumpkins; marshmallow treats take the shape of ghosts. Here's to the fanciful joys of Halloween candy!

*Any situation, no matter how bad, has silver linings.*

*Detach emotionally from the situation and observe it from a bigger perspective.*

*Look at all sides of the situation without judgment.*

*Find positives that might result from this situation.*

*Focus on those positives and how they might improve your life.*

*Go forward in gratitude for the chance to learn a valuable life lesson.*

$\mathcal{L}$ive long enough, and you'll make mistakes. Here's to second chances: at love, at work, in all the machinations of our lives. May we be generous in introducing second chances to others, and may we be open to those granted us. Second chances signify hope.

*Life is short and we have never too much time for gladdening the hearts of those who are travelling the dark journey with us. Oh be swift to love, make haste to be kind.*

—Henri Frederic Amiel

oday I celebrate simple, homespun creativity, within others and myself. Shaping monster faces into the cookie dough. Painting a backyard bench in bright acrylic. Training a pet to do something unusual. I am grateful for creativity, which elevates the ordinary!

When I'm bored, remind me:

This is the excitement of life—

darkness alternating with light,

down dancing with up,

and inactivity being absolutely essential

—as prelude—

to the most fulfilling experiences of all.

It only takes one small act: a smile, an offer of assistance, donation to a charity. When we commit random acts of kindness, when someone shows us kindness, good goes out into the world. We never know when another creature might be suffering; we never know how much a caring act might mean. Let us celebrate kindness and how it elevates us!

Sherri grew up with wealth and privilege. But it didn't stop her from experiencing debilitating depression and anxiety when she got older. The money and glamour wasn't enough to fill the emptiness.

She began a meditation practice that included focusing on ten things she was grateful for. At first, it was all about money and objects, but soon her focus moved to friends, family, her pets, the ocean, and even funny movies. In time, Sherri began to realize she was more grateful for the free things in life, and her depression began to lift.

Our animal companions add so much joy to our lives. Their silly antics charm us. Their trust in us keeps us honest. Their uncomplicated affection warms our heart

In the different stages of their lives, they offer different things— and need different things from us. A playful, energetic kitten spark laughter, while an older animal is a steadfast companion. In taking care of them, we connect to the best part of ourselves

*The one absolutely unselfish friend that man can have in this selfish world, the one that never deserts him . . . is his dog.*

—George Graham Vest

*Happy is the home with at least one cat.*

—Italian Proverb

*The . . . dog, in life the firmest friend, the first to welcome, foremost to defend.*

—George Gordon, Lord Byron

$\mathcal{K}$nitting. It's good for the brain. It's creative. It relieves anxiety. And when you're done with a project, you've created something beautiful and useful. That feels good! After all, if you can, in fact, knit your niece a sweater, who knows what else you might accomplish? Thank you, knitting!

*I*f everything were the same, if all people were the same, life would be boring. Same same same translates into colorless. Without savor. Let us remember how different cultures, different people, different ways of being expand and enhance our own experience. Let us celebrate diversity.

Tomorrow is a dear friend's birthday, and I am excited about the gift I've chosen for her: a scarf made of silvery-blue yarn. I know she'll love it—blue is her favorite color—and the yarn is soft, not scratchy. I am grateful for this opportunity to show her how much she means to me. I honor the joy of gifts given and received!

We didn't exactly see eye to eye

As our friendship teetered and years rolled by

But thanks to the fences you'd always mend

I'm lucky today that you call me friend.

Spiders build webs that are intricate examples of engineering—works of art, even. Bees produce honey and pollinate plants. Ladybugs eat pests, and are therefore loved by gardeners. The insect world gives us many examples of beauty and aid; bugs are a wonder!

*We hope that,*
*when the insects*
*take over the*
*world, they will*
*remember with*
*gratitude how we*
*took them along*
*on all our picnics.*

—Bill Vaughan

*O*ur family includes three cats adopted from local animal shelters. We adore them: funny and loving, even years after adoption our cats seem grateful to have a home. The shelters they hail from are devoted to finding families for animals who've fallen through the cracks; I am so grateful for a system that honors animal life, and which has enriched our lives!

Rita hated the restaurant business. But her parents had owned the little Italian eatery and now they were giving it to her. She knew they thought they were doing a good thing, but she wanted to pursue her writing and didn't want to be tied down to a business.

But the more time she spent going over menus and budgets and dealing with the staff, the more she realized she liked being so emotionally invested in a business, especially one her family started. She even began her own food blog. She felt grateful that her parents had entrusted her with their dream. Now she was a part of that dream too!

When you're sick or in pain, it's difficult to be grateful. But cultivating a habit of gratitude during those times can bolster your spirits and help you maintain your emotional resilience.

Keep an eye out for the medical personnel who are kind, the friend who offers help, or the pharmacist who is prompt and efficient. Let your gratitude for their actions sustain you during difficult times.

When we understand Time to be the Now—a series of Nows that, when combined, form a life—we understand the importance of making the most of the opportunities Time affords us. When we make the most of each Now, when we honor each day, we make our lives—our Time—works of art.

*Good times teach you how to feel contentment.*

*Bad times teach you patience and faith.*

*Joy expands the heart and spirit.*

*Struggles build resolve and character.*

*Love empowers and inspires.*

*Anger fuels change and transformation.*

*Courage leads to great achievement.*

*Fear alerts you to dangers and obstacles.*

*In all things, find grace. At all times, be grateful.*

Education at its best helps us learn to think critically. We learn to manage our time. We learn to do our work individually and as part of a team. Education challenges us to be creative; it opens the world to us. In school, we learn about the past, and we are given tools to help direct the future. Even as we celebrate education, may we strive to ensure it for future generations!

When your spirits are low, look up at the sky. Spot a bird soaring, a plane leaving contrails far above, maybe even a hot air balloon. These things that can conquer gravity can lift your heart as well.

$O$h! I have slipped the

surly bonds of Earth

And danced the skies on

Laughter-silvered wings.

—John Magee

A door repainted.

A recipe rediscovered.

A lost friend refound.

An old song out of the blue.

Gratitude for old things made new.

*W*hen we are children, there are many beginnings: for babies in particular, life is brand new and each day brings its firsts. But even as adults we celebrate beginnings: we greet new seasons, perhaps move to a new home, begin reading the collected works of an author new to us, or bring home a new pet. We are lucky in beginning, all through our lives.

This week I received a handwritten letter. The writer had taken the time to choose a card she knew I'd enjoy; she'd taken the time to write the note, address and stamp the envelope, and find a mailbox. Her efforts warmed me. I appreciate technology, but there is still a place in our world for a practice that brings much joy. I am grateful for handwritten letters.

When I was younger, I had a hot temper and an impatient spirit. Time has mellowed me. Sometimes I look back at that fiery young person and think of all the struggles that could have been avoided had I possessed an even temper. But the years teach their lessons. I am grateful for the patience that comes from life lived.

$\mathcal{D}$ear Mother,

Thank you for the souvenirs

You've given me throughout the years—

Your love, your strength, your faith in me,

And precious childhood memories.

There is no activity we do more in a lifetime than sleep, but scientists still disagree about what it's for. Does it affect memory? Does it clear toxins from the brain? Regardless, we can't do without it: if you're trying to learn something new—like French or a new swim stroke—you'll perform better after you sleep. Some researchers even believe that sleep spurs creativity. We may not fully understand it, but sleep is something to be celebrated!

My daughter, who was a baby when my mother lost her battle with cancer, loves to hear stories about her grandma. I share how my mother was a strong woman, from a strong generation, and how I am grateful for the example she set. Mom's worldview informs the way I parent, and the choices I make every day. Our ancestry is a touchstone even as it informs the future.

Stumbling happens. Don't I know it! I can get bummed out just by reviewing my mistakes and mess-ups from yesterday. But thankfully, I don't need to! My worst blunders, even if they've been truly harmful to myself or others, are not the end of the world. Tomorrow is a new day, a fresh start, a redeemed relationship, a restored soul.

*Life* is rife with mystery, and when we reflect on that mystery, we must come to terms with the fact that not everything in the world can be explained or quantified. With that understanding comes a certain joy, an expansiveness. A little mystery is good for our spiritual selves!

The trait of ambition has gotten mixed reviews over time. But healthy ambition or, as Aristotle put it, "proper ambition," can be a positive, spurring us on to new heights and achievement. Ambition helps us flourish and, when judiciously exercised, can help others flourish, too. Throughout history, ambition has pushed the envelope and changed the world for the better.

It is easy to become discouraged. We spend all day preparing a special meal but then the roast is burnt. We don't get the job offer. We study for the test but don't earn an A. It is persistence that gets us through these setbacks. We get up and move forward. We try again. Let us celebrate persistence, which gets us where we need to go.

$\mathcal{E}$lectricity is a form of energy. Because of it, we can light a lamp on a cold, dark day. We can watch a movie on television, our food stays cool in the refrigerator, and we keep the climate of our homes comfortable. Though we sometimes take it for granted, electricity is something to celebrate: it's wondrous in its power.

*Keep an eye out today for unexpected
bursts of color . . .
A wildflower growing in an
unexpected place
A person in a somber suit wearing
neon green sneakers
A colorful umbrella on a rainy day*

*We may run, walk,*
*stumble, drive, or fly, but*
*let us never lose sight of*
*the reason for the journey,*
*or miss a chance to see a*
*rainbow on the way.*

—Anonymous

*A*bee

staggers out

of the peony.

—Matsuo Basho

Food can be a source of great pleasure: sharing a meal with loved ones helps us connect. The food doesn't have to be fancy. The conversation doesn't always have to sparkle. But we cannot go without food. We are lucky to have it, and the dinner table unites us. We are blessed when we can eat simply and well, together.

Our sense of smell delights us: think homemade bread, or the scent of freshly cut grass. It warns us to look out: when we smell that skunk, it's time to bring the pets indoors! And smell triggers memories: passing a stranger wearing your grandmother's perfume can take you back decades to your grandparents' kitchen and the love you shared. A sense of smell deepens and enhances our everyday experience.

$\mathcal{I}$ appreciate night, bright day's flip side. I love its coolness—the dark velvet skies and sparkling constellations. If the sun burns hot, then the moon is all cool beauty. The world takes a breath. I am grateful for the balance night brings.

*He who does not get fun and enjoyment out of every day needs to reorganize his life.*

—George M. Adams

*A little garden in which to walk, an immensity in which to dream, at one's feet that which can be cultivated and plucked; overhead that which one can study and meditate upon; some herbs on earth and all the stars in the sky.*

—Victor Hugo

It is easy to be consumed by the future or the past. We worry about tomorrow's schedule. We worry about what happened yesterday at work. But when we engage in a hobby, something we love, we can get lost in the moment and really focus on the present moment. Let us find what we love and pursue it; let us dwell in the Now.

*Life is complicated. And technology, for all its wonders, can complicate life further. Texts, emails, our laptops: in a society where we can be reached 24 hours a day, we must work to stay centered rather than fragmented. We must cultivate—and celebrate—a calm heart. When our hearts are serene, we face the distractions of the day with grace.*

$\mathcal{H}$istory—our own, the nation's, the world's—informs us. We can learn from history and improve ourselves. We can read stories of the past and avoid making the same mistakes. We can study leaders from history and strive to emulate their strength. History has much to share; if we are wise, we make it a part of our lives today.

$S$inging releases endorphins, those morphine-like chemicals produced by the body that make you feel happy. Singing also releases oxytocin, a natural stress reliever. It's good for your brain, and has been proven to boost your immune system. So don't be shy: belt out a few tunes and celebrate song!

Natural light holds a lot of sway. As it changes throughout the day, our attitudes, our way of engaging, can be affected. Some people crave the uplift of natural light, and miss it when the seasons turn or storms blow through. And sunlight can positively affect our physical selves, providing vitamin D essential to good health. We recognize the beauty and power of light!

The windows of my soul I throw
Wide open to the sun.

—John Greenleaf Whittier

Give me the splendid silent sun with all his
beams full-dazzling.

—Walt Whitman

They've been compared to diamonds. We organize them into pictures, called constellations, which appear to their best advantage at different times of year, telling stories and even acting as vital navigational tools. They inspire paintings and song. Stars are magic.

The feeling of getting a massage after a long work week.

The joy of your loved ones making you breakfast.

The contentment of a productive day coming to an end.

The first sip of coffee on a cold morning.

The warmth of the sun as you run errands.

The love of a pet that greets you at night.

The precious presence of family and friends.

As children, we grow exponentially. Sometimes there are growing pains; sometimes we seem to sprout an inch overnight. Though we eventually stop growing physically, may we never stop growing altogether. Life invites us to continually bloom spiritually, emotionally, and intellectually; let us celebrate the lifelong adventure of growth!

Having a child late in life wasn't my original plan. Once I realized I couldn't have more kids, I broke down in regret. Why had I waited? It took a lot of meditating to find a blessing in the fact my child would never have a sibling.

But as my child grew, I began to feel grateful for how my life had played out. I got to be more present for my "only" and give him all my time and attention. I realized we were a perfect family just the way we were and I never regretted it again.

$\mathcal{L}$asting love is beautiful to witness. When you're feeling jaded, spend time with an elderly couple whose steadfast love has lasted through decades. See the kindness and caring that has lasted through everything life threw at them.

Two days before her wedding, Danica's old boyfriend showed up, wanting to talk. He was the love of her life, but had left her. She had moved on. Or so she thought. There was much unsaid between them.

Danica met him for lunch and they talked for hours. She felt guilty, but when she left, she realized she'd been protected by not marrying him. He was still shallow and selfish, and she had found a good man she loved. A man who was loyal and loving. She felt a wave of gratitude for the beautiful plan of her life.

oday I am grateful for the wind: the sound of it, its promise of change, the feeling of excitement it creates. When a storm marches in from the west, I like watching how invisible wind arrives first, making itself visible in the movement of trees and scuttle of leaves. The wind tells me that anything is possible!

Research indicates that good family ties help us cope well later in life— kids with strong connections to some sort of family tend to grow up and exhibit resilience in the face of life's ups and downs. And family doesn't have to be blood. Family is the people in our lives who are happy having us in theirs. Family grounds and strengthens us.

$\mathcal{W}$hen we experience loss, we have the opportunity to grow stronger. Loss enhances our appreciation for the given moment, because it helps us understand the fleeting nature of all things. And if we have experienced loss firsthand, we can counsel others because we truly understand. To paraphrase the poet Alfred Lord Tennyson, loss grants us wisdom.

$\mathcal{E}$xperiences shape us. Life's successes and failures, joys and losses, help determine our beliefs and decisions in life. Our experiences have power. If we are wise, we learn from them and constantly grow. Let us honor our experience and the person it has helped us to become.

# Water

Taking a hot shower after a long day

Drinking a glass of cool water on a hot day

Running through sprinklers as a child

Wading in a pond to catch tadpoles

Splashing in puddles

Relaxing in a hot tub

During heat waves, air conditioning can make a difference in terms of not only the comfort, but the safety of old, sick, or frail people. And climate control keeps factories safe for workers who might otherwise be adversely affected by searing temperatures. We appreciate air conditioning because it keeps us comfortable, but it also, arguably, saves lives: now that's cool!

When we are honest—with others, with ourselves—we benefit. We gain the trust of others. Our own self-knowledge and self-esteem are strengthened. When we surround ourselves with honest people, we interact knowing that all parties act with integrity. It can take courage to be honest, and honesty requires tact. Honesty is a powerful, worthy trait.

$\mathcal{W}$e are grateful when we have savings
to draw on for unexpected expenses or crises.
Health, home, education: sometimes the
game changes and we need to rely on savings
to get through this chapter and into the next.
Let us celebrate the resources available to us!

Our pets provide unconditional love that can be a balm to the soul. The feel of a cat's rumbling purr in the morning; a dog's eager welcome at night. These things uplift us. It is good to be needed by our animal friends, to love and be loved in return.

*I remember being told to give thanks in advance for things I wished to see in my life. I thought that was strange, but decided to try it. Interestingly, putting myself in a state of gratitude changed not only my attitude, but the energy I was giving off. Sure enough, doors began to open and people began to respond to me differently.*

*When I am thankful for what I have it seems to move energy back in my favor. Sharing those blessings opens even bigger doors, to happiness and a sense of joy and wonder.*

From the moment we wake, our ears bring us the news. Coffee gurgles, birds sing. We like a new song on the radio. We communicate and are warmed by the voices of those we love. Hearing connects us to the world and reminds us of its many blessings.

*Grateful for breaking my ankle? Seriously? When my friend told me to look for the blessing in my broken bone, I laughed. I had to stop going to the gym and it was a pain to get to work.*

*I wasn't grateful at all.*

*But then . . . it slowed me down enough to see how I was rushing about all the time, often accomplishing very little. It caused me to rest more, which my body needed. In the end, I was grateful, not so much for the broken bone, but for how it made me slow down the hectic pace of life.*

$\mathcal{S}$et aside five minutes and pick a natural object resting nearby. Do nothing but observe this object. Let it become the only thing you are aware of. Look at it as if you had never seen anything like it before.

No one spoke,
The guest, the host,
The white
chrysanthemums.

—Ryota

$\mathcal{G}$iving of ourselves connects us to others. When we are generous to those in need, we forge new social networks. We look outside ourselves, which benefits us even as it puts good into the world. Just as important is to allow others to be generous to us. Let us honor the give-and-take that enriches our lives.

Lily was leaving home for college. She was excited, but afraid. Her parents had always been there for her. Before she left, they threw a party for her, and gave her a car.

She left the next week and missed them like crazy! It was hard being away, until she opened a box that came in the mail. Chocolates and roasted nuts and all her favorite treats . . . and a note saying "Welcome to the treat box of the month club!" Lily was grateful that her parents were always thinking of her. With their love and support, she could do anything.

Though society often sends the message that perfection should be the goal in all things, imperfection has something to teach us. Consider *kintsugi*, the Japanese art of fixing broken pottery. Pieces are repaired with lacquer combined with powdered platinum, silver, or gold, a process that arguably renders an object even more beautiful. The pottery in all its imperfection is seen as enhanced. The cycle of breakage and repair is understood to be something to celebrate, not hide.

My sister was always my best friend.
Growing up, we did everything together.
We dressed alike and shared toys. But in my
20s, we lost touch for a long time. Only over
a decade later did we end up living
in the same town.

We gradually ended up spending more
time together. At first it was awkward, but
soon we were right back where we were as
kids, leaning on each other and being best
friends. I am so grateful circumstances
brought me back to my sister again.

The softness of a pillow, the warmth of a hug. Smooth pebbles underfoot when one wades in a stream. Touch offers comfort, but also warning: I feel the heat of a fire and know not to come too close. I am grateful for senses that connect me to the world.

*How simple and frugal a thing is happiness: a glass of wine, a roast chestnut, a wretched little brazier, the sound of the sea.*

—Nikos Kazantzakis

*Let us be grateful to people who make us happy, they are the charming gardeners who make our souls blossom.*

—Marcel Proust

It can be thrilling to experiment. If you've always prepared eggs sunny side up, try scrambling them one morning. If you usually listen to the local jazz radio station, branch out one day and try a college program. Experimentation keeps us fresh, and our outlooks open. Let us celebrate the growth we enjoy when we move beyond our established comfort zones!

As a child, I never thought much about the presents under our Christmas tree. I assumed it was Santa, and when I knew better, that my parents were rich. I was shocked to find out how poor we had been.

I am grateful that my parents did what they could to provide us the most fun holidays possible. Today I know the power of a child's joy. I do my best to make my son's Christmas the best. My parents sacrificed for us, and for that I will always be so thankful. I try to pay them back daily with the one thing money cannot buy . . . love.

Good neighbors feed the fish and water the plants when you're out of town. They have sugar to lend when you've started baking and realize you've run out. They offer a smile and a wave when you go out the door. Good neighbors create community; they are a blessing.

Marcus was bullied as a kid, and it scarred him. But when his own son was bullied, he was suddenly grateful for the experience—he could now share it with his own child. They had many long talks about how the bullies were hurting, too.

It warmed his heart when his son came home one day to announce he had talked to one of the bullies and befriended him! Marcus realized his lessons had not been lost on his son, and that his own pain could help stop the pain in others. That filled his heart with gratitude.

$It$ hasn't been so very long since Sir Alexander Fleming accidentally discovered penicillin. Sometimes we simply find what we're not looking for: more than 80 years after its discovery, penicillin continues to effectively treat diseases that used to threaten life. Our lives are better, thanks to Fleming's revolutionary discovery!

Friends are always there for you, even when far away.

A true friend knows all your faults, and loves you anyway.

A friend tells it to you straight, but gently so.

Friends make life more fun and less lonely.

You can count on your friends to support you.

Real friends are priceless treasures in human form.

Friends accept you and celebrate you!

$\mathcal{H}$ome means different things to different people. For some, home is part of self-definition, expressed through furnishings or decoration. For others, home is simply wherever their loved ones are. Regardless, home grounds us; it gives us a stable environment to which we return with pleasure, even relief. Home is a haven.

$\mathscr{B}$ecause we live in a fast-paced society, it is easy to feel fragmented. It is common to skim the surface of things, skating over projects or relationships in order to "save time." May we not be spread so thin that we fail to appreciate the nuances of our work, our home, and the people we love. Let us resist the tendency to take the shallow route, and instead pursue depth in our lives.

Reunions with loved ones help us connect to the past that has shaped us; they help us sustain relationships with others over time. Longstanding positive relationships are linked to longevity; when we connect again and again over the years, with people who are important to us, we are sustained. Reunions allow us to feel part of a continuous story.

I rode horses as a child and was once put on a
horse way too advanced for me. I was terrified
and didn't want to leave the paddock area.
I feared being thrown.

But this horse sensed my fear and was
unusually slow and gentle. I learned that
day about communicating with my horse
and actually got out of my comfort zone and
cantered a little. I was so thankful for a horse
that knew how to handle me, and I ended up
riding him once a month afterwards!

$\mathcal{I}$ live near a major city, and am grateful for its bounty: the museums, art galleries, theaters, shops, and restaurants that enlarge my world by introducing me to new experiences. How rich life is, and how many ways there are to live it! The city and its offerings remind me of this, and help me to grow as a person.

*Be grateful for the delicious smells*

*that greet your nose each day.*

*Be grateful for the tastes and textures*

*of your favorite foods.*

*Be grateful for the sensation of sun*

*and wind on your bare skin.*

*Be grateful for the sound of children*

*laughing and birds singing.*

*Look around with your eyes, and see*

*all there is to be grateful for.*

After a long and busy day or week, take time to relax. Quiet time restores our bodies, our souls, and our health. If you can, set aside time each day to let go of your worries and cares and just rest in calmness and peace.

If worries and idle thoughts come to mind, don't try to drive them away—instead, let them come, accept them, and then let them go. Being mindful doesn't mean that you ignore your concerns, but that you stay anchored in the moment.

*Rest and be thankful.*

—Anonymous

*Rest is not idleness, and to lie sometimes on the grass under trees on a summer's day, listening to the murmur of the water, or watching the clouds float across the sky, is by no means a waste of time.*

—Sir John Lubbock

How marvelous to be connected to an extended family! I am so grateful to those who have brought us to who we are today. I am honored to be part of this family.

*Every baby born into the world is a finer one than the last.*

—Charles Dickens

$\mathcal{W}$e have so many things to teach you, little one: how to walk and speak, how to take care of yourself, and how to make good choices in life. But the most important lesson we will ever teach you is this: You are loved.

*The sweetest flowers in all the world—A baby's hands.*

—Algernon Charles Swinburne

Our village hosts a Farmer's Market on Saturdays during the summer. Every week I enjoy the stalls of bright vegetables, crafts, and honey. Some of the merchants have even come to know me; one started setting aside sunflowers once he learned that they are my favorite flower. The colors, tastes, and sense of belonging delight me; I celebrate the Farmer's Market and all it has to offer!

*Surely there is something in the unruffled calm of nature that overawes our little anxieties and doubts: the sight of the deep-blue sky, and the clustering stars above, seem to impart a quiet to the mind.*

—Jonathan Edwards

Books broaden our horizons and provide a door into other times, other worlds. That paperback you've been reading? It might actually be improving your vocabulary (and by extension your writing skills). Books help us improve our focus. They can even reduce stress! Books make our lives better.

*You cannot say you are thankful.*

*You must feel it.*

*You cannot claim blessings without*

*giving blessings in return.*

*You cannot shun pain and hope*

*to experience joy.*

*You cannot avoid challenges and*

*never know the glory of achievement.*

*You cannot exist without affecting*

*those around you.*

*You cannot be alone when you are*

*surrounded by love.*

Where would we be without all the herbs and spices that give our food flavor? The next time you cook, take a moment to savor the smells of the ingredients you're adding in. Cinnamon and nutmeg, mint and rosemary, cumin and ginger—they all add zest to the food we eat.

*The greatest gift of the garden is the restoration of the five senses.*

—Hanna Rion

*My kitchen is a mystical place . . . where the surfaces seem to have significance, where the sounds and odors carry meaning that transfers from the past and bridges to the future.*

—Pearl Bailey

Vegetables and fruits! How often they are dismissed as a boring but necessary evil, when in fact they are something to celebrate. This morning I cut up a plum for my son's lunch, and slipped a slice under my tongue. What a burst of sweetness! And fruits and vegetables are powerful, contributing to my health and well-being. I honor their strength!

After working in the garden yesterday, I was satisfied but grimy: earth had collected under my fingernails, and I was dirty to my elbows! How pleasing it felt to wash up with a cake of lavender soap, which smelled soft and fresh. I feel simple gratitude for the soap that keeps me clean.

Sammy hated going to school in a wheelchair. He was worried about being bullied. Fourth grade was hard enough. He knew he would be walking soon, but for now, he was scared.

When he got to class, a boy sat down next to him and began talking. Sammy was anxious, but soon he was talking back. The boy became Sammy's new friend, and revealed later he'd been in a wheelchair for his entire third grade year. Sammy was grateful. He vowed to befriend anyone he saw alone and lost. By year's end, he had plenty of friends and loved school.

Friends are good for us. Friendships with depth and meaning validate our sense of self, and strengthen our identity as a person who matters. Old friendships draw on years of shared experiences; that's a comfort. With the help of friends, we weather loss, and celebrate joy.

Good conversation can challenge and inspire. It connects us to others, and helps us learn to listen. When we converse, an exchange takes place: of ideas, of values. Engaging in this give and take broadens our horizons: even if we don't agree with another's position, we are forced to defend our own. Conversation helps us grow.

Friendship is a special package—to be
handled with care, to be gratefully acknowledged,
and whose value we should always esteem.

*Happy is the house that
shelters a friend.*

—Ralph Waldo Emerson

It doesn't matter whether our mentor is a parent, a teacher, or a friend. Mentors tell us we are not alone as we grow and learn to cope with life's ups and downs: at school, at work, in day-to-day living. We are blessed by mentors who contribute insights throughout life. A mentor assures us: someone cares.

*M*ovie theaters used to be palaces that created an environment befitting the magic of film. Though contemporary theaters no longer evoke Aztec temples or Italian castles, movies continue to transport us. They tell the story of our world and other worlds; they provide excitement, examine human nature, and provoke laughter and tears. Movies fill us with wonder.

$\mathcal{F}$amily reunions are special times, full of reminiscing, hearing tales from those in the oldest generations, and seeing similarities and differences in the way people talk and think. Stories are shared as food is passed around the table, and laughter abounds.

Newborn babies inspire such gratitude!

The sweet weight of them

Their wide eyes

The sunlight in their smiles

Their tiny, precious fingers and toes

$\mathcal{W}$e start anew at each sunrise. What unique occurrence will happen today that may never happen again? What can we be thankful for this day, this, hour, this moment?

*Yosemite Valley, to me, is always a sunrise, a glitter of green and golden wonder in a vast edifice of stone and space.*

—Ansel Adams

When we daydream, we look to the future and the past. Our creativity gets a jumpstart, and sometimes the solution to a seemingly insolvable problem becomes clear. Honoring the time to reflect helps us stay tuned to what's important to us. May we always make time to dip into ourselves and dream.

Nana's death was painful to the whole family. Everyone had loved her. When her will was read, several of those loving family members turned on each other out of greed. I didn't care if Nana left me anything. I had memories and I was grateful for those.

She did leave me an old book called "A Dog of Flanders." It was tattered and yellowed, but I loved it as a child. Nana cherished that book. I am most grateful to have it because it means I meant something to her. Something special.

*Day One: Write down five things good that happened today.*

*Day Two: Meditate on one thing you love that makes your heart sing.*

*Day Three: Treat yourself to one small indulgence without guilt.*

*Day Four: Be good to your body and exercise and eat right.*

*Day Five: Commune with nature and feel how connected you are to life!*

No one likes disappointment, but it's essential to personal growth. Through disappointment, we learn resilience. We learn what we care about—if we didn't care about something, we wouldn't be disappointed, right?—and how to recover from setbacks. May we learn to embrace disappointment, which spurs us to creatively make—or remake—our way in the world.

*L*ive today in such a way

That when tomorrow comes,

The memories of yesterday

Will all be cherished ones.

On most mornings, in most parts of the world, we need only stick our heads out the window to hear birdsong. Morning after morning they are out there, declaring a mysterious joy.

*Never give up listening to the sounds of birds.*

—John James Audobon

The cheerful birds their airy carols sing,
And the whole year is one eternal spring.

—Ovid

*The smallest birds sing the sweetest; it is always pleasant to hearken to their songs.*

—James Fenimore Cooper

*The birds with their plumage and their notes are in harmony with the flowers.*

—Henry David Thoreau

*W*here would we be without our elders—those hardworking parents, grandparents, and forebears who made such amazing sacrifices? It is good to remember what they did and how they lived.

*If nothing is going well,*
*call your grandmother.*

—Anonymous

Your family may be less than ideal, but they are your family. It was more than luck that brought you together. Faith and forgiveness, kindness and cooperation, laughter and love— these will preserve the precious bonds between you.

*Working in the garden can be a meditative activity. It feels good to move the earth. We weed and we plant; the air is fresh. Sometimes we grow vegetables, and the salad that results tastes like spring. Gardens are good for the soul.*

$\mathscr{L}$iving in harmony with nature's seasons awakens us to spring's renewal, fall's cozy slowness, winter's savory rest, and summer's exuberance. Thus we are reminded to honor each season's energies for the wisdom they hold.

*P*hotographers celebrate the golden hour, that magical time shortly after sunrise or before sunset when daylight has a particularly mellow glow. When we start the day in a wash of golden light, when the day ends in warm, syrupy radiance, our hearts lift. The next time you are out when the sun is setting, take note. The golden hour can inspire.